For my fellow self-identifying billionaires,

Not all of us were born into this world a billionaire. But at one point in our lives, self-identifying billlionaires such as myself, Bill Gates, Elon Musk, and Jeff Bezos all realized this non-billionaire body we were born in wasn't who we truly were. This led us all at some point to take the steps to begin our transition to become a billionaire. While some transitioned faster than others, some of us still have yet to complete our transition and suffer from the dysphoria every day of having to live in a non-billionaire body. I simply seek the euphoria of being the true billionaire I am. That is why I have included a new ending in this Billionaire Edition of my book exclusively for my fellow self-identifying billionaires. I hope this new ending not only reminds us how special we are, but inspires my fellow self-identifying billionaires to help those of us who have yet to complete our transitions.

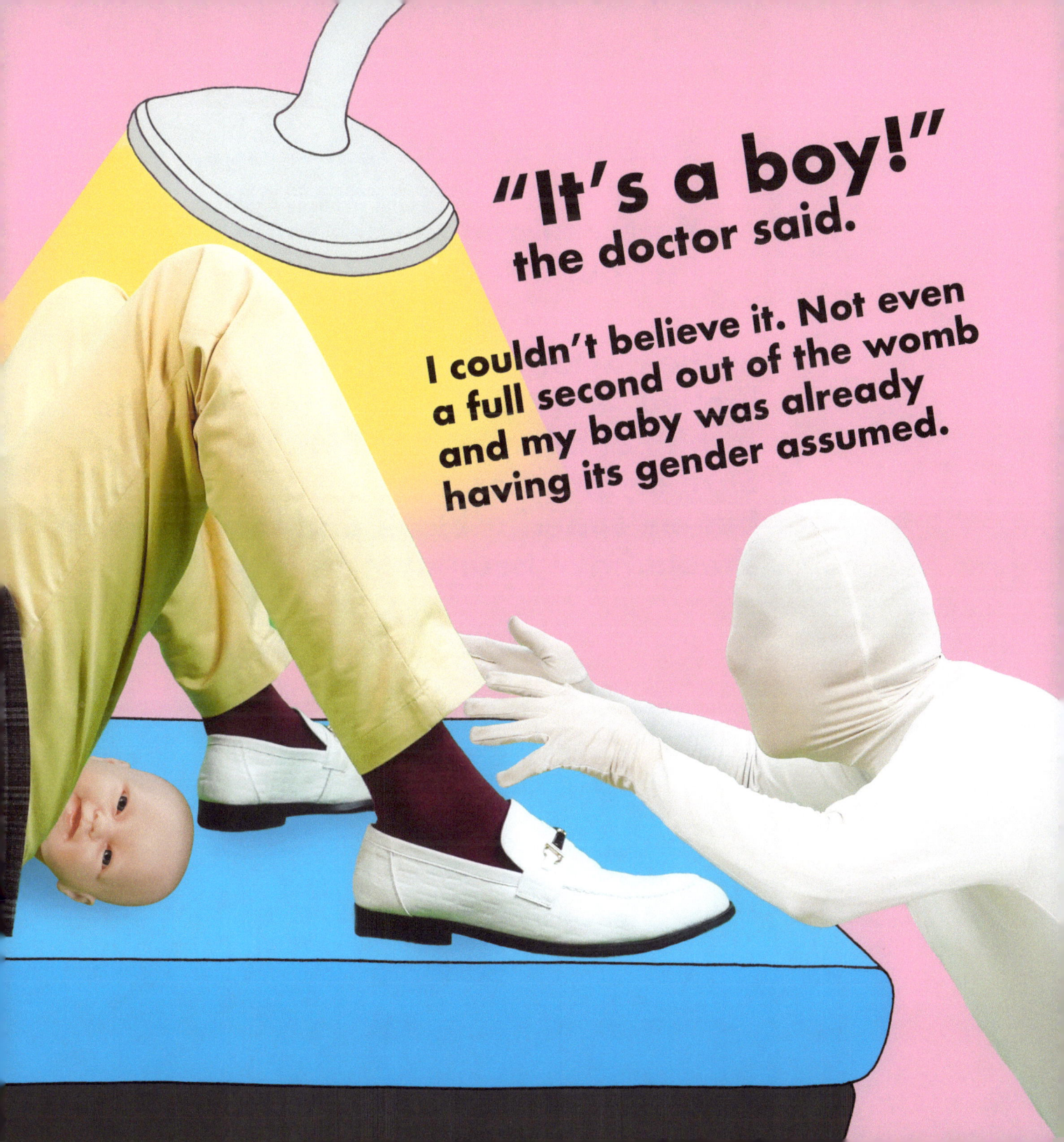

"It's a boy!" the doctor said.

I couldn't believe it. Not even a full second out of the womb and my baby was already having its gender assumed.

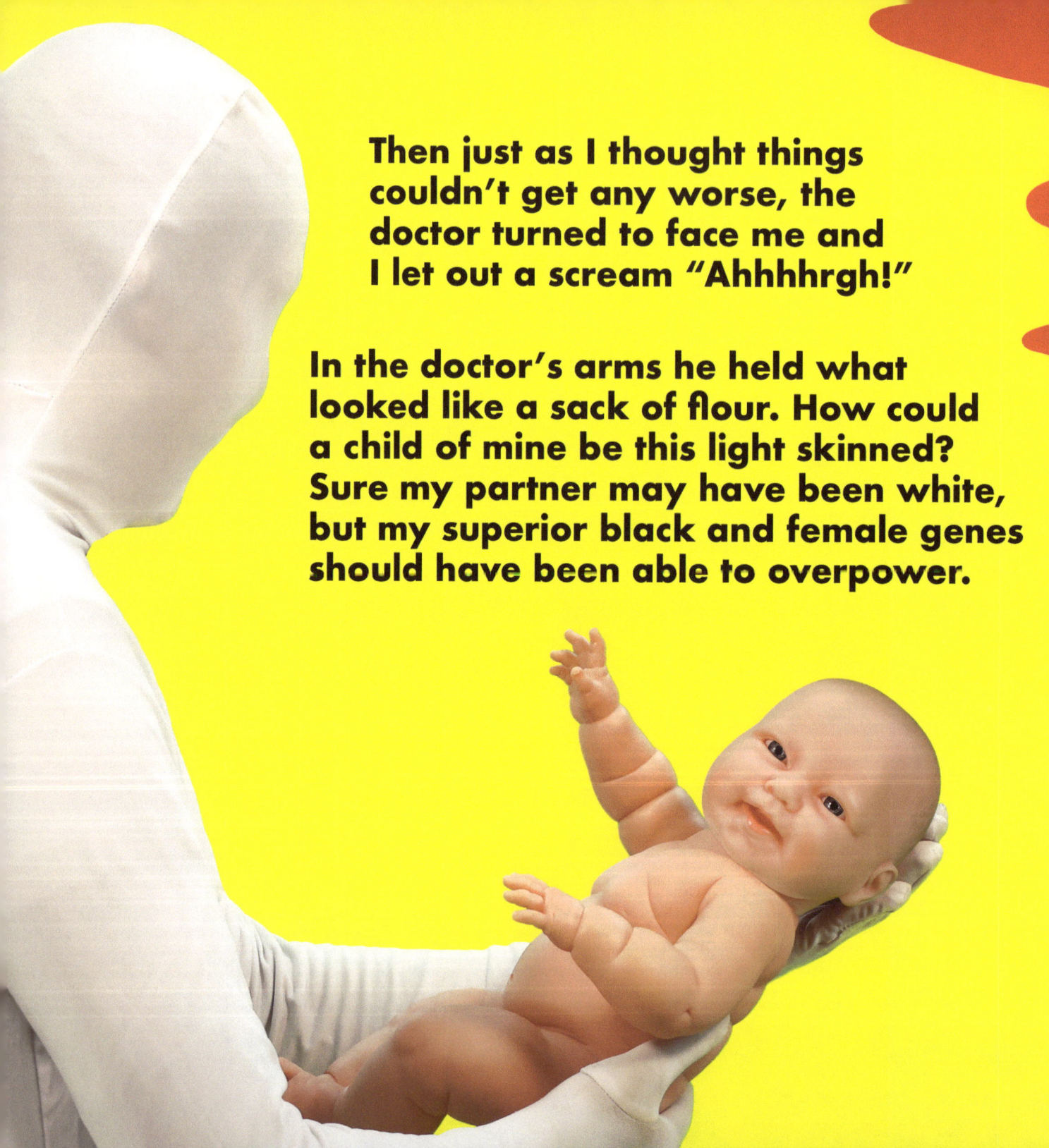

Then just as I thought things couldn't get any worse, the doctor turned to face me and I let out a scream "Ahhhhrgh!"

In the doctor's arms he held what looked like a sack of flour. How could a child of mine be this light skinned? Sure my partner may have been white, but my superior black and female genes should have been able to overpower.

I couldn't take the abuse anymore. I grabbed the baby and threw the doctor to the ground and ran.

But then out of nowhere something happened that would change my life forever. As I ran through traffic, all of a sudden I tripped and the baby flew from my arms.

The baby whooshed and soared through the air. Its body flying with the grace of an eagle, but spinning with the trajectory of a football towards the end zone.

Sploosh! The baby landed in a puddle by a sewer drain. The impact of the baby's oversized buttocks against the water made a splash so massive it hit me in the face. I wiped the water from my eyes, revealing a sight that made my heart stop.

Before me was a baby laying in the most fierce, the most iconic, and the most feminine pose I had ever seen. As my baby lay with its wrist flicked with the sass only a black woman could possess, it was in that moment I suspected you, my child, identified as female.

But being the responsible mother I was, I had to be sure. So the next day I found a Jewish rabbi on Craigslist to have you circumcised. Snip. Slash. Squish. Splash. With each cut of your penis I happily stared, knowing if you ever transitioned you were now part way prepared.

Then as I eagerly watched the rabbi finish the circumcision ritual by placing your penis in his mouth to suck it clean, the sudden joy your face was overcome with was my second clue.

But the moment I knew for certain was when I tried to breastfeed you. As I undid my shirt you began to cry, refusing to latch onto my nipple. It was clear you had a distaste for females and therefore could not be a straight male.

All that was left for me to do was prove to a doctor you identified as a female and not a gay male. So I conducted a test. On the floor I laid out a woman's thong and some man's boxer briefs. Then I let you go.

Inch by inch you crept closer and closer. Inside all I could feel was the thump, thump, thump of my heart beating like a drum. I watched you crawl and fall. You shifted right and then left, left and then right.

You were signalling to me you wanted the female artifact inside of you. Because the fact was, inside of you was a female trapped in a male body. I had to free my girl from her shell. So I grabbed the baby and ran.

"Finish what you started!" I told the doctor. The doctor informed me he had suffered a fractured neck in our last encounter and was not fit for surgery. "You brought my baby into this world, now you must bring my girl into this baby!"

The doctor refused. I then forced him to watch footage of the gender test I had conducted. But again, the doctor refused.

"If you don't do it then you're a transphobe and I'll tell your boss to have you fired!" I shouted. The hair on the back of the doctor's neck quickly stiffened. He slowly turned and looked me in the eyes, "P-p-please don't! I'll do anything".

So the doctor called in his doctor friends and they began. They snipped and they snapped. They cut and they shut. They injected and corrected. Then finally after a full day's work, my baby girl was finally her true self.

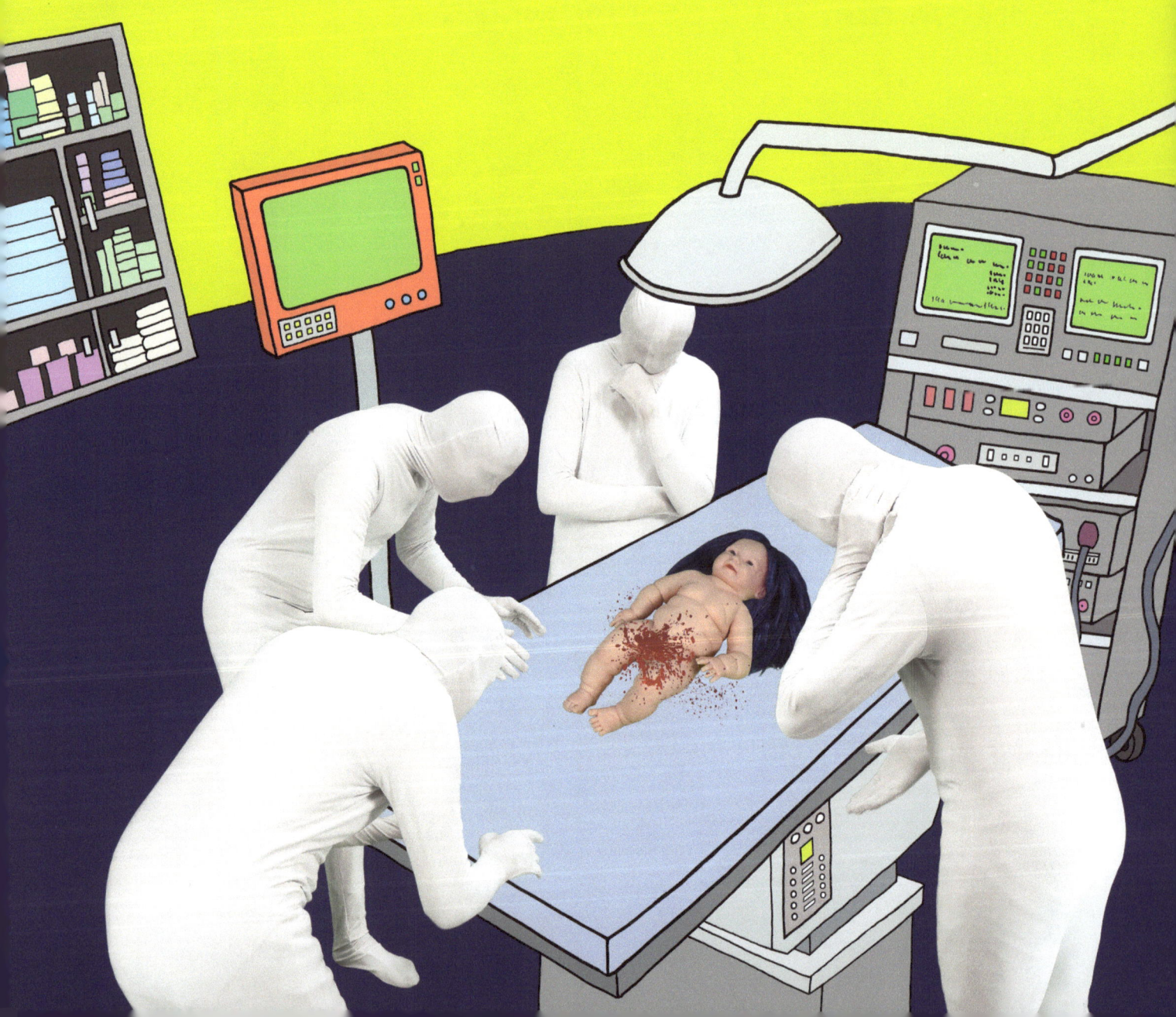

That night me and my girl danced and we gossipped. We giggled about boys and played with my toys. But something just wasn't right. Her skin was still a sin.

I tried everything to bring out her true color. In the mornings I had her bake in the sun. In the afternoons we played catch with charcoal.

And in the evenings I made her sleep in a box full of coffee beans. But the next day she'd wake up the same pale color.

Then one day as I lay in the sun, contemplating whether to give up and have an abortion, I heard a noise "ahm-ahm-ahm". I didn't see anything so I laid back down. Then I heard the noise again "ahm-ahm, ahm-ahm".

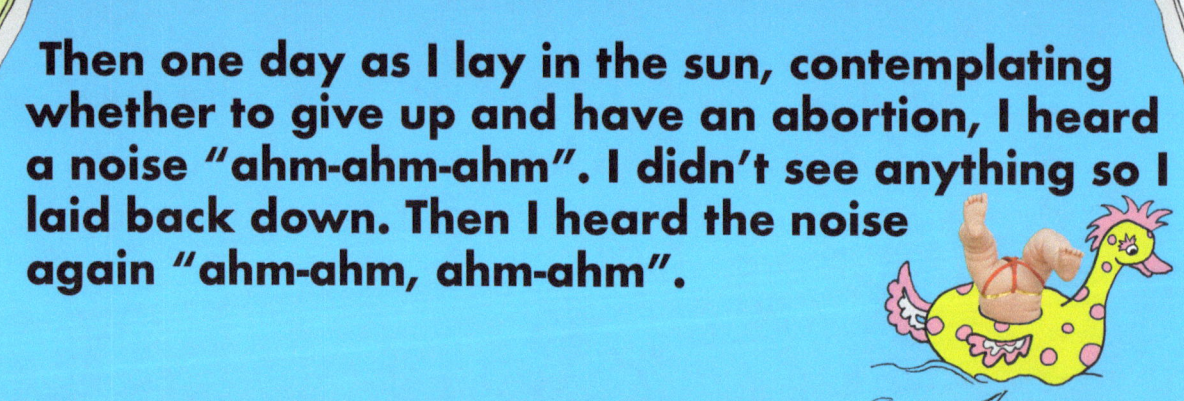

I thought perhaps I was going crazy from dehydration so I reached for my glass of water. But as I looked through the glass, I saw my baby laying in the sun alone on the other side.

That's when I heard it again. The sound was coming from my baby. But it wasn't saying "ahm-ahm, ahm-ahm", I realized it was saying "mama, mama".

I walked over and as I bent down to pick up my baby, suddenly the world stopped and it finally hit me.

I had been so focused on what my baby wasn't, that I had forgotten what my baby was. Sure my baby may not have been dark skinned, but still my baby was non-cis, non-white and non-male. And that was enough to make my baby her mommy's girl.

Just then out of nowhere I heard a "beep, beep" coming from my front yard. Before me were a dozen men unloading a truck full of cash. I felt a tap on my shoulder and I turned around. "Mam, on behalf of the government, we are ready to finally pay for your transition to become a billlionaire."

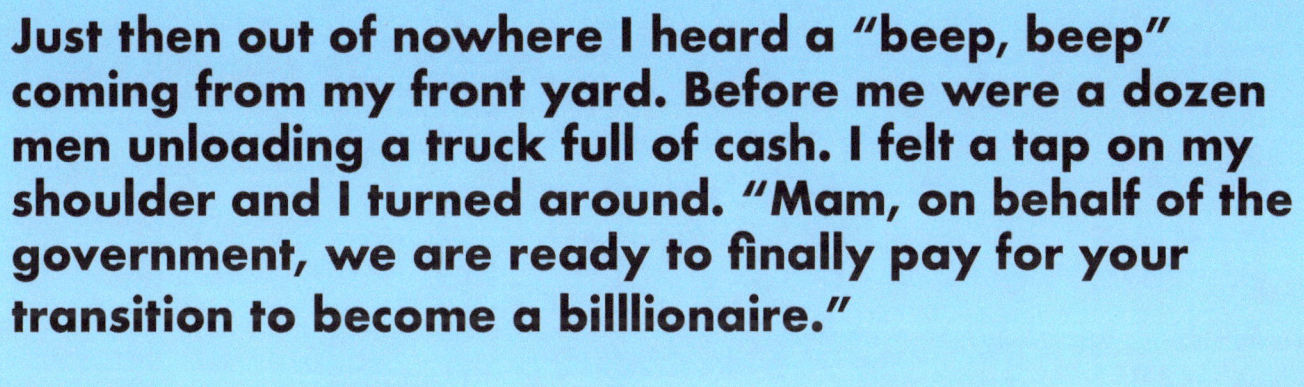

THE END.

WARNING:

The certificate on the next page is ONLY available for those eligible who have watched the entirety of my full Woke Training Film, which can be seen at "Freshtastical.com" (or Youtube.com/Freshtastical)

Copyright © 2022 Spencer Cathcart

All rights reserved. No part of this book may be reproduced or transmitted in any form or by any means, electronic, mechanical photocopying, recording or otherwise, without prior written permission of the author and sole copyright owner Spencer Cathcart.

Text Copyright © by Spencer Cathcart
Illustrations Copyright © by Spencer Cathcart

ISBN: 978-1-7386794-1-6 (Regular Edition)
ISBN: 978-1-7386794-0-9 (Billionaire Edition)

www.freshtastical.com

www.ingramcontent.com/pod-product-compliance
Lightning Source LLC
Chambersburg PA
CBHW041705160426
43209CB00017B/1753